Dear Judy.
This was given to me
...in good faith. Hope y...
use it wisely.
Love Aunt Betty.

Published by

WELLTON BOOKS

P.O. Box 989
Citrus Heights, Ca.
95610

ISBN 0-943678-03-X

—Printed in U.S.A.—

Can hardly wait for an invitation to a good home cooked meal. John Andrew.

COOKING IN THE NUDE®

"For Women Only"

Written and illustrated by
Debbie & Stephen Cornwell

Cooking in the Nude, For Women Only is the fun and playful approach to the art of culinary seduction. Whether you're planning an evening of tasteful teasing or delicious decadence, our romantic recipes are sure to inspire your endeavors!

Our format and style can be as tempting and suggestive as you need to fit the occasion. Whatever your objectives are, enticing entrees such as **"Flaming Passions"** or **"Appledesiac"** are certain to make your point. After all, each dining experience in *For Women Only* is intended to show off your best assets, and help you find his!

BE ADVISED: The authors assume no responsibility for any overreaction on the part of your dining companion. Prepare these risque recipes only if you are over 21 and fully understand their potential!

We encourage you to maneuver your man with our menus and be **"Less Than Subtle"** with each entree. **"Don't Stop Now"** with vegetables and neither will he! Your liberated sense of humor and our sensual innuendo will put you on top in the gourmet game!

TABLE OF CONTENTS

TURN ON DE'LIGHTS

(Creating the mood)

An evening of culinary seduction can be as romantic and loving or, as sensual and lusty as you like. How you play out your role of epicurean temptress probably depends more on what your objectives are *after dinner*, than during the meal itself! But, whether you plan to end the evening at the front door, in the bedroom, or somewhere in between, we're going to assume that *you* will be the aggressor tonight!

Someone once said that the hardest task for a woman, is to prove to a man that his intentions are serious. Just how serious *you* wish his intentions to become depends, of course, upon your own desires! Depending on the circumstance, your motives could range from an evening of mild flirtation to a blatantly seductive weekend! Maybe you only want to captivate him for the next few hours or, perhaps your objectives are longer term. Either way, keep one important thought in mind; there's no such thing as a dangerous woman, only a susceptible man!

Because men are especially susceptible to visual stimulation, you can "Turn On De'lights" and encourage whatever response you want. Show off an elegant and suggestive table setting with low lights, or candles, to maneuver your man's libido. Manipulate his fantasies with flowers, soft music, and his favorite apertif. You're the aggressor. Do you have him where you want him yet? Perhaps, but, men aren't always the greatest when it comes to noticing the obvious and sometimes, this requires a less than subtle approach.

We knew of a woman whose man owned his own business and worked long hard hours. He came home late each night, never noticing the candles and flowers, much less his lady. Obviously, a less than satisfying arrangement. Finally one evening, she greeted him at the door, wearing only a lace camisole, and offered him a glass of his favorite wine. She promptly hid his briefcase and escorted him to the den where she had replaced the business magazines with, shall we say, more provocative publications. Thirty minutes later, she served a simple, yet elegant dinner and, we're told, they finally fell asleep around 3 A.M. the next morning! Although she has never repeated this performance, we understand he now arrives home from work an hour earlier each evening!

6

Now we don't mean to imply that many situations require such an aggressive approach. After all, your dinner guest may be someone who has sparked your interest, but, has never even been to your home before tonight. It all gets back to your own intentions for the evening's encounter. Maybe you want him to leave, after dinner, thinking of you as a liberated, interesting, and sexy conversationalist that he would like to see more of (the pun was intended!). If that's your motive, a little verbal teasing, low lights, (but no candles) and an entree like "Flaunt Your Fillet" may be the way to go. If *he* turns out to be liberated, interesting, and sexy, you can always invite him back for "A Naughty Proposition", complete with candles!

When you think *he's* right, Turn On De'lights! Send him enticing visual messages but, don't forget the other four senses. Your preparation in the kitchen and your own perfume will penetrate and excite his sense of smell. The right background music, along with your teasing and suggestive comments, will titillate his audio senses. You can Bait The Trap further with appetizers, a good wine and finally, your entree, to tantalize his sense of taste. As for teasing his sense of touch...we'll leave that up to you!

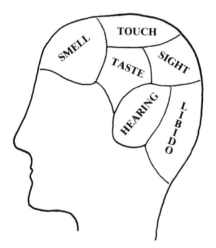

TIGHT JEANS

...and other pantry needs

When it's time to "slip into something more comfortable" you can turn to your wardrobe for tight jeans, slinky silk, or lacy lingerie, to fit the occasion. Your pantry should be as varied and as ready for each endeavor of epicurean teasing! As with your wardrobe, a limited assortment could restrict your results. Be as lavishly prepared to go all the way (or as far as you want) with any of our entrees! Give yourself all the options with a well rounded pantry containing the following:

brandy
calvados
Drambuie
madeira
orange flavored liqueur
  (curacao or Grand Marnier)
port
scotch
sherry
tequila
triple sec
vermouth
dry white wine
  (sauterne, if possible)
dry red wine

anchovy fillets
artichoke crowns
diced green chilis (canned)
jalepeno chilis (canned)
clam juice
liver pâté
phyllo leaves

arrowroot
basil
bay leaves
caraway seeds
chervil
cinnamon sticks
marjoram
nutmeg
paprika
saffron
sage
sesame seeds
tarragon
thyme

almonds
pine nuts
walnuts
raisins

SHRIMP BALLS

1 HOUR

STEP ONE:

8 oz. cheddar cheese, grated
6 oz. raw shrimp, cleaned,
  deveined, finely chopped
1 T. diced green chiles
  (canned)
½ t. seedless jalapeno
chiles, minced

Combine all ingredients and mix well. Form into bite-size balls. (At this point, you may cover and refridgerate until ready to use.

STEP TWO:

peanut oil (for frying)

Heat oil in frypan until almost smoking.

STEP THREE:

1 C. flour
½ C. cornstarch
¾ t. baking powder
  salt, to taste
1 C. water
2 T. vegetable oil
  Japanese bread crumbs
  fresh parsley sprigs

Mix all dry ingredients together. Add ½ cup water and oil, whisking until blended. Continue to add water until batter is consistency of pancake batter. Dip shrimp balls into batter (allowing excess to drip off), then roll in bread crumbs. Fry them, several at a time, until golden brown. Drain on paper towels. Arrange on serving tray with parsley sprigs as garnish.

HOT CRAB DIP

45 MINUTES

2 8 oz. packages cream
   cheese
½ C. mayonnaise
¼ C. sherry
8 oz. crab meat
1 clove garlic, minced
1 t. prepared mustard
french bread, cut into
   bite-size cubes

Preheat oven to 300°. Blend all ingredients well and pour into baking dish. Bake for 45 minutes. Pour into fondue pot or chafing dish and adjust flame to low. Arrange french bread in basket and serve with fondue forks.

FETA CHEESE SPREAD

20 MINUTES

3 oz. feta cheese
8 oz. cream cheese
1 T. sour cream
3 T. minced leek
1 small clove garlic, minced
½ t. dill
¼ t. oregano
¼ t. chervil
¼ t. marjoram
1 T. minced parsley
½ C. chopped black olives

Blend feta cheese, cream cheese, and sour cream together. Add remaining ingredients, except olives, and blend well. Fold in olives. Spoon into serving bowl or crock, cover, and chill. Serve with broken wasa bread or unsalted crackers.

SPINACHEEZ

1 HOUR

STEP ONE:

1 10 oz. package frozen
   chopped spinach, thawed
   and squeezed dry
1 T. butter
¼ C. minced leek
⅓ C. feta cheese
⅓ C. minced parsley
¼ t. dill
1 egg, beaten
   salt and pepper, to taste

Melt butter in frypan over medium flame. Saute leek until tender. Mix in spinach, turn into bowl. Add feta, parsley, and dill and mix well. Blend in eggs, salt and pepper.

STEP TWO:

½ C. butter, melted
1 package phyllo leaves

Preheat oven to 425°. Lightly butter baking sheet. Place one leaf of phyllo on work surface, cut into 2'' wide strips, brush with butter. Cover all but one strip with wax paper, then with damp towel. Place a teaspoon of filling on end of phyllo leaf and fold over and over, forming a small triangle. Brush with butter and place on baking sheet. Repeat with remaining phyllo strips. Work quickly. When finished, brush all triangles with butter and bake for 15 minutes.

STEP THREE:

fresh dill sprigs
cherry tomatoes

Arrange triangles on serving tray. Garnish with dill and cherry tomatoes. Serve hot.

GREENS WITH ENVY

The visual stimulation created by your salad is only limited by your imagination and fantasies. Excersize your free spirit in salad composition by breaking all the 'rules'. Why should lettuce be the primary ingredient——we might play like rabbits, but we don't have to eat like them. A few greens can become the sensual canvas for a titillating offering of anything from pasta and scallops garnished with nasturtium to shrimp and baby mushrooms with asparagus tips. Bridge the gap between the appetizer and entree with a unique presentation which suggests the fantasies that lie ahead.

Hot Crab Dip

Insatiable Greens
with snowpeas and melon

Sea Nymph Mania

Mushroom Madness

Lemon Rice

Chardonnay

SEA NYMPH MANIA

Show him what kind of sea nymph you really are, if you don't have a beach, suggest the hot tub after dinner!

30 MINUTES

STEP ONE:

1 bunch spinach, washed, stems removed. Set aside
¾ lb. fresh ocean scallops
2 T. flour
2 T. butter
1 T. olive oil

Melt butter and oil in frypan over medium-high flame. Put flour in plastic bag and add scallops, shaking until lightly coated. Add scallops to pan and saute until golden and just firm. Transfer scallops to warmed plate, cover loosely, keep warm.

STEP TWO:

2 T. pinenuts (shelled)

Meanwhile, toast pine nuts in 350° oven until lightly browned, stir occasionally.

STEP THREE:

2 T. minced leeks
½ C. madeira
¾ C. whipping cream
2 T. brandy
1 t. fresh lemon juice
dash nutmeg

Add leeks to frypan and saute 1-2 minutes. Add madeira, simmer until liquid is reduced by half. Add cream and whisk until slightly thickened. Reduce flame to low and add remaining ingredients. Return scallops to pan and heat through.

STEP FOUR:

paprika

Divide spinach leaves into two au gratins (or serving dish), top with scallops, nap with sauce. Sprinkle with toasted pine nuts and paprika. Serve immediately.

15

BARING YOUR SOLE

...could lead you to baring more than you bargained for!

35 MINUTES

STEP ONE:

1 lb. petrale sole fillets
salt, to taste
1 C. dry sherry

Preheat oven to 400°. Place fillets in single layer in flameproof baking dish, season with salt. Pour sherry over fillets, cover with foil and bake 10-15 minutes, or until fillets are opaque. Transfer fillets to warm au gratins (or plates), cover loosely and keep warm. Place baking dish over medium-high flame and reduce liquid to ⅔ cup.

STEP TWO:

2 T. butter
¼ C. minced leek
½ C. whipping cream
3 T. orange liqueur
(curacao, Grand Marnier)
grated orange peel from
half an orange

Melt butter in frypan over medium flame and saute leeks until tender. Add fish liquid, cream and orange peel. Bring mixture to a boil, reduce flame and simmer 5 minutes. Nap fillets with sauce and serve immediately.

Spinacheez in Phyllo
Suggestive Salad
with Kiwi and Pecans

Baring Your Sole

Broccoli L'Orange
French Bread
Gerwurtztraminer

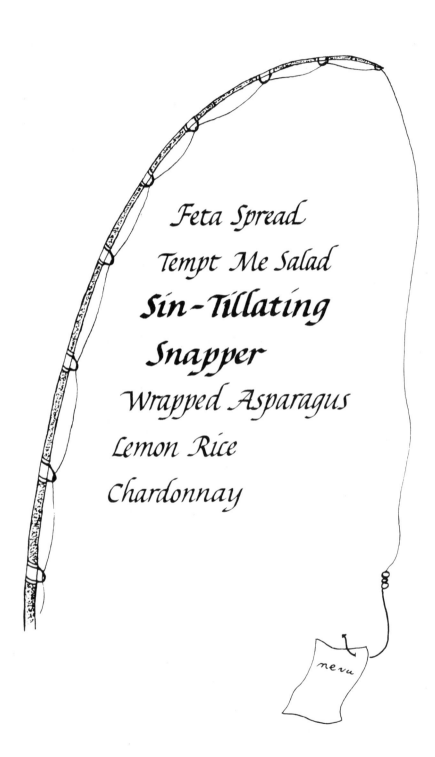

Feta Spread

Tempt Me Salad

Sin-Tillating

Snapper

Wrapped Asparagus

Lemon Rice

Chardonnay

SIN-TILLATING SNAPPER

*...is sinfully delicious; after tasting your wares,
he'll fulfill all your wishes.*

50 MINUTES

STEP ONE:

1 leek, finely chopped
½-1 lb. snapper fillet
salt and pepper, to taste
⅔ C. dry white wine
⅔ C. vegetable broth
(or chicken broth)

Preheat oven to 400°. Butter a large flame-proof baking dish and sprinkle bottom with leek. Arrange snapper in single layer over leek and season with salt and pepper. Add wine and broth to dish. Place dish over medium-high flame and bring to a boil. Cover with foil and bake 10-15 minutes, or until snapper loses its translucency. Remove snapper to warm plate, cover loosely, and keep warm.

STEP TWO:

⅔ C. whipping cream
salt and pepper, to taste

Place baking dish over high flame and boil until liquid is reduced to approximately ½ cup (about 5 minutes). Reduce flame to medium and add cream, cooking until sauce coats the back of a spoon. Add salt and pepper.

STEP THREE:

½ C. finely chopped carrot
½ C. finely chopped celery
½ C. finely chopped leek
2 T. brandy
2 T. madeira
2 T. port

Combine all ingredients in a small saucepan and cook over high flame until liquid is evaporated. Blend vegetables into cream sauce, spoon over fish and serve.

MON PETITE AFFAIR

Sometimes the best things come in small packages!

50 MINUTES

STEP ONE:

2 T. tequila
2 T. triple sec
2 T. sugar
4 T. grated orange peel
2 T. water

Combine all ingredients in a small saucepan and bring to a boil. Reduce flame and simmer 3-5 minutes or until peel is glazed. Set aside.

STEP TWO:

½-1 lb. med. raw shrimp, cleaned and deveined
1 C. dry vermouth
2 T. tequila
1½ T. butter

Combine all ingredients in large frypan and bring to a boil, while stirring. Simmer the shrimp until firm (1-1½ minutes). Remove shrimp to a warm plate, cover loosely, and keep warm.

STEP THREE:

1 T. minced leek
2 T. white wine vinegar
3 T. dry white wine
6 T. orange juice
1 T. grated orange peel
½ C. butter, sliced

Reduce the shrimp liquid, over medium-high flame, to ¼ cup. Add remaining ingredients, except butter, and bring to a boil, reduce to ¼ cup. Reduce flame to low and whisk in butter, one piece at a time. Sauce should be the consistency of light cream.

STEP FOUR:

2 t. minced parsley or chopped chives

Arrange shrimp in heated au gratins (or serving dish). Spoon sauce over shrimp and top with glazed peel. Sprinkle with parsley and serve immediately.

Spinacheez in Phyllo
Scandalous Salad
with mandarian oranges & raisins
Mon Petite Affair
Creamy Spinach
French Bread
Chenin Blanc

Hot Crab Dip
Show Off Salad
Flaunt Your Fillet
Creamy Spinach
Fumé Blanc

FLAUNT YOUR FILLET

Show off your best assets and you're sure to find his!

1 HOUR

STEP ONE:

¼ C. minced onion
3 T. butter
10-12 mushrooms, sliced
4 tomatoes, chopped
½ C. madeira

In frypan, over medium-low flame, melt butter. Add onion and saute until limp. Add mushrooms and cook, stirring occasionally, until liquid from mushrooms has evaporated (approximately 15 minutes). Add tomatoes and madeira, increase flame to medium and cook until almost all liquid evaporates (approximately 15 minutes).

STEP TWO:

2 salmon fillets
3 T. butter
salt and pepper, to taste

In large frypan, melt butter over medium-high flame, add salmon and saute 2-3 minutes per side until it is opaque. Remove salmon to warm plate, cover loosely, and keep warm.

STEP THREE:

¾ C. dry white wine
1 C. whipping cream
2 T. minced parsley
lemon wedges

Pour off remaining butter in pan, add wine and boil until it is reduced to 1-2 tablespoons. Add cream and continue to reduce until sauce is thickened slightly; add 1 T. parsley. Place salmon fillets in au gratins (or on a serving platter). Spoon sauce over salmon, sprinkle with remaining parsley and garnish with lemon wedges. Serve immediately.

23

FLAMING PASSIONS

*Fan his fires with your desires
and get all you can tonight!*

45 MINUTES

STEP ONE:

½ lb. fresh ocean scallops
¾ lb. medium prawns,
  cleaned and deveined
4 T. butter
¼ C. scotch
½ C. Drambuie

In large frypan, melt butter over medium over medium flame. Add prawns and scallops, tossing to coat with butter. Add scotch and Drambuie, warm for 15 seconds and ignite with a match. Turn heat to low and shake pan until flames disappear. Remove prawns and scallops to warm plate, cover loosely, and keep warm.

STEP TWO:

¼ C. bottled clam juice
⅓ C. fresh peas (or thawed
  frozen peas)
⅓ C. julienned carrots
⅓ C. julienned rutabaga

Whisk clam juice into pan, add vegetables, and bring to a boil over medium-high flame. Boil until liquid is reduced by half (approximately 6 minutes).

STEP THREE:

1 T. fresh lemon juice
  salt & pepper, to taste
1½ C. fresh spinach leaves,
  washed, stems removed

Adjust flame to medium-low, add remaining butter to pan, 1 tablespoon at a time, whisking until melted. Add lemon juice and seasonings. Add prawns, scallops and spinach. Cook until spinach is just wilted. Serve in warmed au gratins or serving platter.

Shrimp Balls
Sinful Salad
Flaming Passions
Wrapped Asparagus
Sauvignon Blanc

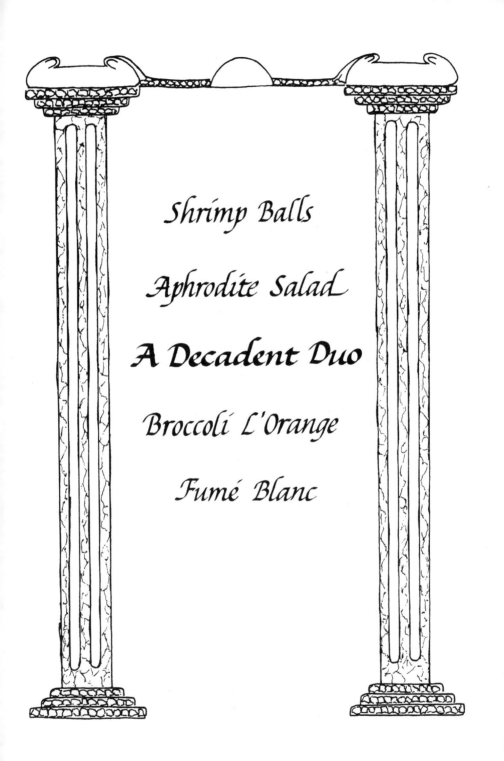

Shrimp Balls

Aphrodite Salad

A Decadent Duo

Broccoli L'Orange

Fumé Blanc

A DECADENT DUO

*...is what we could be, I'll indulge you tonight
and let you please me!*

30 MINUTES

STEP ONE:

2 T. butter
2 T. minced leek
2 T. flour
salt and pepper, to taste
dash nutmeg
⅔ C. milk
½ C. half & half
2 T. dry white wine
¼ C. swiss cheese, grated
2 T. parmesan, grated

Melt butter over medium-low flame and saute leek until transparent. Turn flame to low, add flour, whisking constantly, for 2 minutes. Add seasonings, milk and half & half. Whisk until sauce thickens. Add wine and cheeses, whisking until sauce is smooth, and not too thick (add half & half to thin, if necessary), keep warm.

STEP TWO:

2 slices white bread,
crusts removed
2 T. butter
4 thin slices ham

In frypan, melt butter over medium flame and brown bread lightly on both sides. Place bread in warmed au gratins (or serving platter) and top with ham slices.

STEP THREE:

1½ T. butter
¼-½ lb. lump crab meat
salt and pepper, to taste
2 T. chopped chives
or minced parsley

Melt butter in frypan, add crab, season to taste and saute until heated through. Divide the crab over the ham and nap with sauce. Garnish with chopped chives or minced parsley.

GREAT LEGS

I only have thighs for you!

50 MINUTES

STEP ONE:

6-8 chicken legs, skinned
1 T. butter, melted
2 T. minced parsley
¼ t. thyme
2 T. lemon juice
1 C. chicken broth

Preheat oven to 400°. Lay legs in baking dish (rounded side up). Brush legs with butter and sprinkle with herbs. Mix lemon juice and broth and add to dish. Bake uncovered, 30 minutes. Baste occasionally.

STEP TWO:

3 slices bacon, chopped
  to ½" pieces
1 thick slice white bread,
  cut into ¼" cubes

Meanwhile, cook bacon slowly in frypan over low flame, until golden brown. Remove and drain on paper towels. Increase flame to medium. Add bread cubes and fry until golden; drain on paper towels.

STEP THREE:

2 T. butter
3 T. flour
⅓ C. milk
  salt and pepper, to taste

Remove chicken from dish, reserving liquid, and arrange in warmed au gratins (or serving platter). Melt butter in frypan over medium flame. Whisk in flour and cook 2 minutes. Whisk in milk and reserved cooking liquid. Bring to a boil, reduce flame and simmer 2-3 minutes. Season and sprinkle the bacon and bread cubes over the chicken. Serve immediately.

Spinacheez in Phyllo
Sexy Salad
with avocado and papaya
Great Legs
Mushroom Madness
Lemon Rice
Gerwurtztraminer

Feta Spread

Exhibitionist Greens

Strut Your Stuff

Wrapped Asparagus

Chardonnay

STRUT YOUR STUFF

...and see what he does for you!

1 HOUR 30 MINUTES

STEP ONE:

4 T. chopped marinated
artichoke crowns.
1 T. of marinade reserved
⅓ C. chopped black olives
¾ C. grated monterey jack
cheese

Combine all ingredients, blending well.

STEP TWO:

2 chicken breasts, boned
skinned and pounded to
¼" thickness

Stuff breasts, roll and secure with string or toothpicks. Cover with wax paper and refridgerate for 30 minutes.

STEP THREE:

½ C. flour
1 egg, beaten
1 C. fine dry bread crumbs

Preheat oven to 350⁰. Dust chicken with flour, dip in egg, roll in breadcrumbs. Place in au gratins (or baking dish) and bake for 20 minutes.

STEP FOUR:

3 T. butter
½ t. basil
½ t. fresh minced parsley
½ t. chervil
⅓ C. dry white wine
¼ C. chopped black olives

Meanwhile, melt butter over medium flame, add herbs and wine. Bring to a simmer, reduce flame and keep warm. When chicken rolls are done, pour wine mixture over chicken and continue to bake for 10 minutes more. Sprinkle rolls wih olives and serve.

INSATIABLE

Too much of a good thing can be wonderful!

1 HOUR

STEP ONE:

2 T. butter
6 large mushrooms, sliced
2 T. flour
  salt and pepper, to taste
¼ C. milk
¼ lb. crab meat
⅓ C. swiss cheese, grated

Melt butter in frypan over medium-high flame. Saute mushrooms until tender and moisture has evaporated (approximately 8-10 minutes). Whisk in flour, salt and pepper; cook 2 minutes. Whisk in milk until smooth. Add crab and cheese, blend well.

STEP TWO:

2 chicken breasts, skinned, boned, pounded to ¼" thickness

Spread crab mixture on breast, roll up and secure with wooden toothpicks or string.

STEP THREE:

3 T. flour
½ t. paprika
¼ t. salt
2 T. butter
½ C. dry white wine

Combine flour, paprika and salt. Roll chicken in flour to coat evenly. Melt butter in frypan over medium flame, add chicken and brown evenly. Add wine to pan, reduce flame, cover, and simmer 15-20 minutes.

STEP FOUR:

2 T. flour
1 T. water
2 t. grated lemon peel

Remove chicken rolls to warmed au gratins (or serving platter). Blend flour and water in small jar and whisk into sauce. Continue to whisk until sauce thickens. Spoon over chicken and garnish with lemon peel.

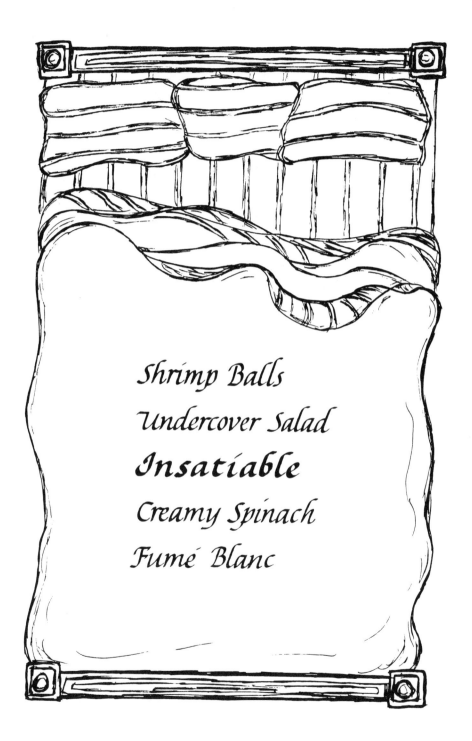

Shrimp Balls
Undercover Salad
Insatiable
Creamy Spinach
Fumé Blanc

Hot Crab Dip

Casablanca Salad
with hearts of palm

**Poulet it Again...
...With Me**

Broccoli L'Orange

Fumé Blanc

POULET IT AGAIN, WITH ME

Romance and intrigue are the keys!

1 HOUR 15 MINUTES

STEP ONE:

3 T. butter
1 medium leek, minced
1 large carrot, minced
8 large mushrooms, minced
salt & pepper, to taste

Melt butter in frypan over medium-high flame. Add leeks, saute 1 minute. Add carrots and mushrooms; continue to saute until most of the moisture from the mushrooms has evaporated. Add seasoning.

STEP TWO:

4 large spinach leaves

Dip spinach leaves in boiling water until barely limp (approximately 5-10 seconds). Drain on paper towels.

STEP THREE:

2 chicken breasts, boned, skinned, and pounded to 3/8" thickness
2 thin slices procuitto ham, or other smoked ham

Lay 1 slice ham over each breast. Lay 1-2 spinach leaves over ham. Spread 2 T. mushroom mixture over spinach. Roll breasts up, secure with toothpicks. Cover with wax paper, refridgerate 30 minutes. Remove toothpicks.

STEP FOUR:

3 T. flour
salt & pepper, to taste
1½ T. oil

Mix flour, salt, and pepper on plate. Flour breasts lightly. Heat oil in frypan over medium flame. Add rolls seam-side down, brown on all sides. Place rolls in au gratins (or baking dish), bake at 375° for 6-8 min.

STEP FIVE:

1 T. olive oil
1 T. butter
1 C. minced mushrooms
¼ t. minced garlic
1 T. minced leek
½ C. whipping cream
1 T. dry sherry
2 t. snipped chives

Heat oil and butter in frypan over medium flame. Saute mushrooms, garlic and leek until limp and most of the moisture has evaporated. Add cream and sherry, increase flame and whisk sauce until thickened. Spoon over chicken, sprinkle with chives.

35

A PASSIONATE PAIR

...in any affair, can do whatever they dare. Dare him!

25 MINUTES

STEP ONE:

¼ C. minced leeks
1 T. vegetable oil
½ C. peeled, chopped
    tomatoes
1 T. madeira
    sugar, to taste
    salt and pepper, to taste

Heat oil in frypan over medium flame, add leek and saute until tender and golden. Add remaining ingredients. When mixture has begun to simmer, turn flame down and keep warm.

STEP TWO:

2 chicken breasts, boned,
    skinned and pounded to
    ¼" thickness
1 T. vegetable oil
1 T. butter
2 thin slices procuitto ham,
    or other smoked ham

Heat butter and oil in frypan over medium-high flame. Saute chicken breasts, turning once, for approximately 3 minutes. Remove to warmed au gratins (or serving platter). Add ham to pan and cook, turning, until it begins to brown. Lay one slice ham over each chicken breast.

STEP THREE:

2 slices mozzarella
2 T. minced parsley

Heat broiler. Lay one slice of cheese over each breast. Broil until cheese melts and begins to bubble. Spoon tomato mixture over breasts. Sprinkle minced parsley over tops and serve immediately.

Hot Crab Dip

Passion Fruit Salad

A Passionate Pair

Mushroom Madness

Garlic Bread

Reisling

Feta Spread
Tight Jeans Greens
Pâté His Filet
Broccoli L'Orange
Pinot Noir

PÂTÉ HIS FILET

...and he'll never stray!

50 MINUTES

STEP ONE (SAUCE):

1 T. butter
3 T. minced leek
1 slice bacon, diced
1 T. flour
1 t. catsup
4 lg. mushrooms,
   stems chopped
½ C. & 2 T. beef stock
¼ C. red wine
   salt and pepper, to taste
1 t. minced parsley
½ t. thyme
½ t. marjoram

Preheat oven to 350°. Melt butter in frypan over medium-low flame. Add leek and bacon, cooking slowly until golden. Add flour, whisking constantly for 2 minutes. Add catsup, chopped mushrooms, stock, wine and seasonings. Bring to a boil, simmer 15 minutes. Add parsley, thyme and marjoram. Continue to simmer 2-3 minutes. Strain through sieve, pour into serving dish, keep warm.

STEP TWO:

1 T. butter
   salt and pepper, to taste

Meanwhile:
Put mushroom caps in buttered dish. Dot with butter and season with salt and pepper. Bake in oven 8-10 minutes.

STEP THREE:

2 slices bread, trimmed to
   same size as filets
½ C. oil
1 T. butter

Melt butter and oil in frypan over medium flame. Fry bread on both sides until golden. Drain on paper towels. Place in warmed au gratins (or dinner plates).

STEP FOUR:

2 filet mignons 1-1½" thick
1 can pâté de foie gras
parsley sprigs

Either barbeque filets or brush with melted butter and broil 5-8 minutes per side. Lay filets on bread. Top each filet with a slice of pâté and 2 mushrooms. Spoon sauce over each filet. Garnish with parsley sprigs. Serve immediately.

39

A NAUGHTY PROPOSITION

...is hard to say 'no' to, so be prepared to carry out your end of the bargain.

40 MINUTES

STEP ONE:

¾ C. walnuts	Using blender or food processor, make walnuts into a paste (approximately 7 minutes).

STEP TWO:

4-6 veal loin chops, boneless **salt and pepper, to taste** **2 T. butter**	Pat veal dry, season both sides with salt and pepper. Melt butter in frypan over medium flame. Add veal and brown lightly (approximately 3 minutes per side). Remove veal to warm plate, cover loosely, and keep warm.

STEP THREE:

½ C. dry white wine **½ C. whipping cream** **½ C. beef broth** **¼ C. brandy**	Pour off fat from pan. Add wine and bring to a boil, stirring in brown bits from pan. Boil until liquid is reduced to a glaze (approximately 2-3 minutes). Blend in cream, broth and brandy. Boil until liquid is reduced by half. Reduce flame to low, whisk in 3 T. walnut paste (adding additional paste, if necessary, to taste).

STEP FOUR:

¼ C. walnut halves **1 T. chopped chives**	Spoon sauce over medallions and garnish with walnut halves, sprinkle with chives.

Spinacheez in Phyllo

Lusty Leaves

with grapes and apples

A Naughty Proposition

Creamy Spinach

Lemon Rice

Chardonnay

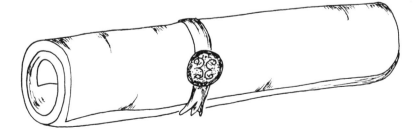

Hot Crab Dip
Adventurous Greens
Vealing Daring?
Mushroom Madness
Lemon Rice
Fumé Blanc

VEALING DARING?

Take a risk tonight and
cast HIS fate to the wind.

45 MINUTES

STEP ONE:

4 veal loin chops, boneless
¼ C. flour
  salt and pepper, to taste
3 T. butter
1 T. olive oil

Put flour, salt and pepper in a large plastic bag. Add veal chops, one at a time, shaking to coat. Melt butter and oil in frypan over medium-high flame. Add veal chops and brown on both sides. Remove veal to plate.

STEP TWO:

½ C. minced leeks
1 clove garlic, minced
8-10 mushrooms, sliced
½ C. madeira
½ C. beef broth
2 t. tomato paste
¼ t. thyme
½ t. marjoram
½ t. sage
1 bay leaf

Add leeks and garlic to pan, saute for 1-2 minutes. Add mushrooms and continue to saute for approximately 6-7 minutes. Add madeira and boil for 1-2 minutes. Add remaining ingredients and bring to a boil. Return veal to pan, reduce flame to medium-low and simmer for 10-12 minutes. Transfer veal and mushrooms to warm au gratins (or serving platter), cover loosely, and keep warm.

STEP THREE:

3 T. butter, cut into pieces
2 T. minced parsley

Skim fat from pan. Turn flame to high and boil until sauce is slightly thickened. Whisk in butter, one piece at a time. Spoon a little sauce over veal and garnish with parsley.

43

BEEFCAKE FANTASY

*As Mae West once said, "It ain't the men in
your life, it's the life in your men!"*

1 HOUR

STEP ONE (BROWN SAUCE):

1 T. vegetable oil
1 leek, chopped
½ medium carrot, chopped
¾ C. beef broth
1 C. water
3 T. chopped parsley
1 bay leaf
¼ t. thyme
2 t. arrowroot dissolved in
   4 t. cold water

Heat oil in frypan over medium flame. Add leek and carrot, saute 5-8 min. Add remaining ingredients, reduce flame to low, simmer 20 min. Strain liquid, skim fat. Return to pan, bring to a boil; reduce to 1 cup. Turn flame to medium, whisk in arrowroot until sauce is thickened, approximately 1 min. Set aside.

STEP TWO:

2 ribeye steaks, boned and
   pounded to ⅓" thickness
1 T. vegetable oil
¾ C. dry red wine
⅓ C. minced leek
¼ t. thyme
1 bay leaf

Heat oil in frypan over medium high flame. Brown steaks 45 sec. to 1 min. per side. Remove steaks to warm plate, cover loosely, keep warm. Remove fat from pan. Add wine. Turn flame to high; add remaining ingredients. Continue to boil until reduced to ¼ cup.

STEP THREE:

1 orange, peeled and
   divided into segments
2 T. butter

In small frypan, melt butter over medium flame; add oranges and saute 3-4 min. Set aside.

STEP FOUR:

2 T. butter
2 t. chopped chives
2 t. minced parsley
½ t. tarragon
   pinch of sugar
   sprigs of parsley

Strain wine into brown sauce, boil until thickened slightly. Reduce flame to low, whisk in butter, add remaining ingredients. Spoon sauce over steaks. Garnish with orange segments and parsley sprigs.

44

Shrimp Balls
Cute Tush Salad
with artichoke bottoms
Beefcake Fantasy
Wrapped Asparagus
Merlot

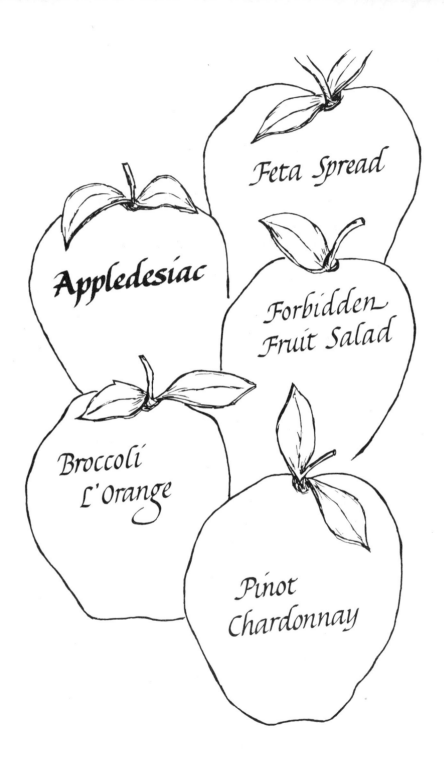

Feta Spread

Appledesiac

Forbidden
Fruit Salad

Broccoli
L'Orange

Pinot
Chardonnay

APPLEDESIAC

You're not the first to use apples, but, you may be the best. Find out tonight, put him to the test!

1 HOUR 20 MINUTES

STEP ONE:

1 T. butter
1 large apple, peeled, cored and cut into rings ½" thick
2 T. calvados

Melt butter in frypan over medium-high flame. Add apples, turning to coat. Saute 3-4 min., or until firm and golden. Add calvados to pan, heat for 10-15 sec., ignite. Turn heat to low, shake pan until flames die. Remove apples and set aside. Reserve liquid.

STEP TWO:

2 1-1½" thick boneless pork loin chops, well trimmed (fat reserved)
2 T. calvados
⅓ C. apple cider
¼ t. sage
¼ t. thyme
¼ t. marjoram
pepper, to taste

Place fat in clean frypan over medium flame. Render until there is enough melted fat to cook chops. Remove any pieces of fat from pan. Add chops to pan and brown well (approx. 5 min. per side). Pour off any excess fat; add calvados. Turn heat to low, ignite. When flame dies, add cider and seasonings. Cover and simmer 30 min.

STEP THREE:

Preheat broiler. Remove chops to au gratins (or serving platter). Overlap apples on top of chops. Add reserved apple cooking liquid to pan. Turn flame to high; boil until reduced to a syrup (2-3 min.). Brush syrup over apples and broil 2-3 min.

STEP FOUR:

½ C. whipping cream
salt, to taste

Whisk cream into syrup. Turn flame to high; boil until sauce is thickened slightly. Season. Nap chops with sauce; serve.

HOT HUNK RIBS

Find out just how hot your hunky guy can be!

3 HOURS 30 MINUTES

STEP ONE:

1 side pork spareribs, cut into 2-rib pieces
1½ t. salt
1 t. paprika
1/8 t. pepper

Preheat oven to 325°. Lay ribs in baking dish. Sprinkle with salt, pepper and paprika. Bake, uncovered, for 30 minutes. Turn ribs and continue to bake for 30 minutes. Drain off fat.

STEP TWO:

¼ C. chopped onion
¼ C. water
1 apple, shredded
1 potato, shredded
1 lb. can sauerkraut
caraway seed

Add onion and water to ribs. Combine apple, potato and sauerkraut, place over and around ribs. Sprinkle with caraway and continue to bake for 1½-2 hours. Turn ribs and sauerkraut occasionally to keep from drying out.

STEP THREE:

1 T. butter
1 large apple, cored and cut into ½" rings

Melt butter in frypan over medium flame. Add apples and saute until golden, but still firm. When ribs are done, remove sauerkraut to warmed serving platter. Top with ribs and garnish with apple slices and parsley sprigs.

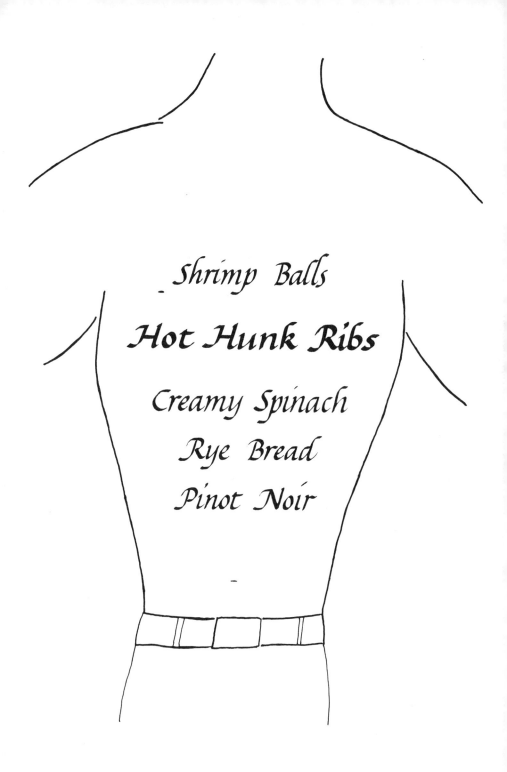

Feta Spread

Voyeurs Salad

I Only Have
Eyes For Ewe

Creamy Spinach

Lemon Rice
Zinfandel

I ONLY HAVE EYES FOR EWE

Let's leave the lights on tonight!

2 HOURS

STEP ONE:

1½ lb. breast or leg of lamb cut into bite-size cubes.
1 T. olive oil
1 T. butter
1 clove garlic, minced
½ t. rosemary, crushed
pinch sage
salt and pepper, to taste

Melt butter and oil in frypan over medium-high flame. Add lamb and brown on all sides. Add remaining ingredients and blend well.

STEP TWO:

1 T. flour
½ C. dry red wine
½ C. vegetable broth

Mix flour and ½ T. wine to form a paste. Add remaining wine, whisk into lamb. Add broth, whisk over medium-high flame until slightly thickened. Reduce flame to low, simmer 1½ hours.

STEP THREE:

1 recipe lemon rice (page 59)

About 30 min. prior to end of cooking time for lamb, cook rice.

STEP FOUR:

1 T. butter
6-8 large mushrooms, sliced

About 10 min. before lamb is done, saute mushrooms over medium high flame, until tender. Add to lamb.

STEP FIVE:

2 t. anchovy paste or 2 anchovy fillets, mashed

Remove ½ cup sauce from lamb; blend with anchovies, return to pan. Simmer 5 min.

STEP SIX:

½ lemon, sliced, each slice with a cut from center to outer edge, then twisted

Spoon lemon rice into warmed au gratins (or around edge of serving platter. Mound lamb in center and garnish with a twisted lemon slice on top.

IN LUST AGAIN

...and again, and again...

35 MINUTES

STEP ONE:

3-4 lamb tenderloin chops, 1-1½" thick, boned, well-trimmed of fat
salt and pepper, to taste
1 t. rosemary, crushed
3 T. flour
1 T. butter
1 T. olive oil

Season both sides of chops with salt, pepper and rosemary, dust with flour. Heat butter and oil in frypan over medium flame. Brown chops well on both sides, 3-5 minutes per side. Remove chops to warm platter, cover loosely, keep warm.

STEP TWO:

4-6 cloves garlic, minced
½ C. dry white wine
½ C. beef broth
½ t. rosemary, crushed
½ C. whipping cream
2 T. butter

Add garlic to pan, saute over medium flame until golden. Whisk wine into pan, add beef broth and rosemary. Bring to a boil and reduce by half. Whisk in cream, boil until thickened. Whisk in butter, one piece at a time. Add juices from platter and blend.

STEP THREE:

6 cherry tomatoes
2 T. chopped chives or minced parsley

Remove chops to warmed au gratins (or serving platter), nap with sauce and garnish with tomatoes and chives.

Feta Spread

Alluring Leaves

In Lust Again

Mushroom Madness

Gamay Beaujolais

1 lust/^{n} **a:** pleasure, delight **b:** personal inclination **c:** intense longing **d:** eagerness

2 lust/^{v} **a:** to have intense desire or need **b:** craving, wanting

Shrimp Balls

Ewe Turn Me On

Broccoli L'Orange

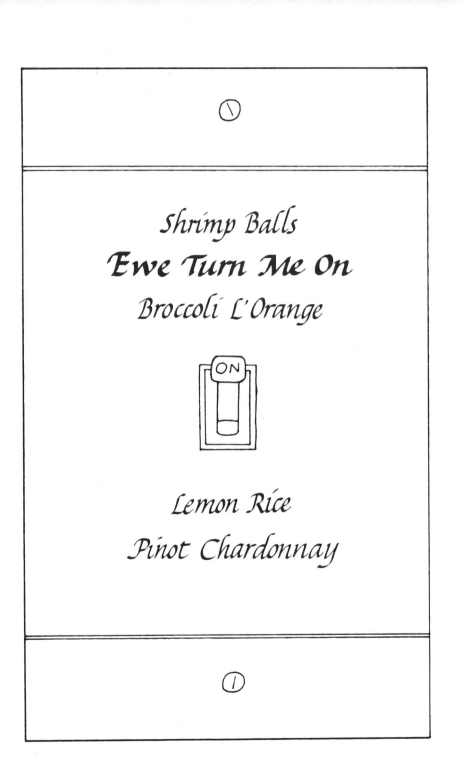

Lemon Rice

Pinot Chardonnay

EWE TURN ME ON

...but, will I still lust you tomorrow. Let's find out!

2 HOURS

STEP ONE:

1½ lb. lamb breast or
shoulder, cut to bite-size
cubes
salt and pepper, to taste
1 medium onion, minced
½ C. beef broth
¼ t. ground saffron, or
saffron threads
1 small cinnamon stick

Season lamb with salt and pepper. Melt butter in large frypan over medium-high flame. Add lamb and onion. Saute until onion is tender and lamb is browned. Heat broth in small pan, add saffron, stir until dissolved. Blend broth into lamb. Add remaining broth and cinnamon. Reduce flame to low and simmer 1½ hours.

STEP TWO:

½ C. blanched whole
almonds

Meanwhile, place almonds in single layer in pie pan and toast in oven at 350° until lightly browned (approximately 10 minutes). Stir occasionally.

STEP THREE:

1 T. honey
1/8 t. cinnamon
½ C. raisins

Remove lamb to bowl. Discard cinnamon stick. Add honey and cinnamon and simmer 5 minutes. Return lamb to pan. Add raisins and simmer 5 minutes.

STEP FOUR:

toasted almonds
sesame seeds

Spoon lamb into warmed au gratins (or serving platter) and sprinkle with almonds and sesame seeds.

55

MUSHROOM MADNESS

25 MINUTES

STEP ONE:

½ C. proscuitto ham, diced
1 T. olive oil
¼ C. pine nuts

Add oil to large frypan, over low flame, lightly brown proscuitto. Remove to small bowl. Add pine nuts to pan and increase flame to medium. Saute until golden and remove to small bowl.

STEP TWO:

1 T. olive oil
1 clove garlic, minced
1 leek, minced
½ lb. mushrooms, sliced
3 large mushrooms, minced

Reduce flame to low, add oil if needed. Saute garlic and leeks until tender. Increase flame to medium-high. Add all mushrooms and saute, stirring frequently, until mushrooms just begin to lose their juices.

STEP THREE:

2 T. madeira
2 T. whipping cream
2 T. minced parsley

Add madeira and boil until liquid is reduced to 2 tablespoons. Add cream, reduce flame to low and cook until sauce thickens. Stir in parsley, ham and pine nuts. Serve immediately.

HAM WRAPPED ASPARAGUS
IN CREAM SAUCE

40 MINUTES

STEP ONE:

8-10 asparagus spears,
  trimmed to 7"
2 slices ham,
  2" x 6" x 1/8"

Steam asparagus until just tender. Divide asparagus into two servings. Wrap a slice of ham around middle of spears and lay seam-side down in baking dish.

STEP TWO:

1 large egg
¾ C. whipping cream
2 T. swiss cheese, grated
2 T. parmesan cheese,
  grated

Preheat oven to 350⁰. Blend egg and cream. Pour over asparagus bundles. Sprinkle with cheeses. Bake. 25-30 minutes, or until cream is set and cheeses are golden brown.

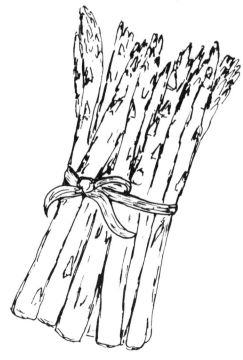

BROCCOLI IN ORANGE BUTTER

20 MINUTES

STEP ONE:

1 head broccoli,
  broken into florets
½ C. orange juice

Steam broccoli until just tender. Meanwhile, in small saucepan, over medium-high flame, reduce orange juice to 2 tablespoons.

STEP TWO:

4 T. butter
1 T. grated orange peel
1 T. minced leek

Melt butter in frypan over medium-low flame. Add leek and orange peel. Saute until tender. Blend orange juice into leeks. Add broccoli and toss gently to coat. Serve immediately.

CREAMED SPINACH
40 MINUTES

STEP ONE (CREAM SAUCE):

2 T. butter
2 T. flour
1¼ C. milk
salt and pepper, to taste

Melt butter in frypan, over medium-low flame. Whisk in flour and cook 2-3 minutes. Whisk in milk and bring to a boil. Add salt and pepper and remove from heat.

STEP TWO:

¼ C. finely ground salt pork
¼ C. minced leek
1 10 oz. package frozen spinach, thawed and squeezed dry
salt and pepper, to taste
½ C. cream sauce

In frypan over medium flame, saute salt pork until browned. Add leek and saute until translucent. Add spinach, salt and pepper, stirring until completely heated through. Add cream sauce, cover and cook over low flame 20-25 minutes. Stir occasionally.

LEMON RICE
25 MINUTES

1 C. cooked rice
1 egg
2 T. lemon juice
2 T. grated parmesan cheese
salt and pepper, to taste
2 T. minced parsley

Prepare rice. Just before serving, combine remaining ingredients in bowl and mix well. Stir mixture into hot rice and blend well.

INDEX

ON A SCALE OF ONE TO TEN

ON A SCALE OF ONE TO TEN